Tales of Tenali Rama

Wit • Wisdom • Humour

Retold by:
Jyotsna Atre

Illustrated by:
Chandan Sen Gupta

Contents

I.S.B.N.: 81-780-6067-1 © Publishers

Published by: **UNICORN BOOKS Pvt. Ltd.,** J-3/16,Darya Ganj, New Delhi-110002

Phones: 23276539,23272783/84, Fax: 23257790, E-mail: unicornbooks@vsnl.com

Introduction

In the early sixteenth century, King Krishna Deva Raya ruled in the southern parts of India. A just and learned ruler, Krishna Deva Raya was also known for his quicksilver temper. During his iron reign, Vijayanagara became one of the most powerful and prosperous empires of south India.

Krishna Deva Raya was also a great connoisseur of arts and literature. His court was filled with wise and talented men from all walks of life. But his favourite courtier, undoubtedly, was the court jester Tenali Rama. A young man with sharp wit and acute intelligence, Tenali Rama was famed as one of the eight pillars of the Vijayanagara court, although his brilliant sense of humour often found him at war with the other courtiers. But Tenali would always use the right word and the right action and invariably, escaped the most perilous situation with his gift of brains and jest.

Tenali Rama was of humble origins. Named Ramakrishna at birth, he grew up at his maternal uncle's house in a small village called Tenali. So, people began to call him Tenali Ramakrishna or simply Tenali Rama. As Tenali grew in stature, he displayed a strong sense of justice and empathy for the common man. While his witticism and humour endeared him to Krishna Deva Raya, his sense of fair play earned him a place in the hearts of the people.

So popular are the stories of his sharp intellect that they have been passed down for generations, turning Tenali Rama into a legend that lives on.

The Royal Heir

The seven identical boys stood before the King of Vijayanagara. The same manner, the same age, the same height, the same hair, the same clothes... Who were they?

"I come from the great kingdom of Kalinga, O King," the old man bowed before Krishna Deva Raya. "My Lord, your old friend the Emperor of Kalinga, sends his son, the royal heir, to visit Vijayanagara."

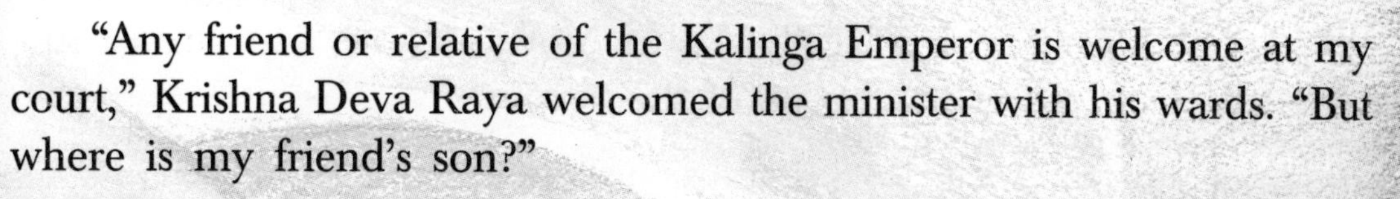

"Any friend or relative of the Kalinga Emperor is welcome at my court," Krishna Deva Raya welcomed the minister with his wards. "But where is my friend's son?"

"One among these seven boys is the Prince, My Lord," the minister presented the boys to Krishna Deva Raya. "But he may not reveal himself. His father, the King of Kalinga, has set you a riddle."

Krishna Deva Raya smiled. "So typical of my dear friend!" He looked around his court of eminent scholars. "But there is no puzzle that my courtiers cannot solve." He turned to the Kalinga minister. "Ask them your question, learned one."

"The question is fairly simple, Sire. Which one of these boys is the Prince of Kalinga?"

"Why, that's easy!" responded the Prime Minister. "Any astrologer can easily tell that by reading the palms of the seven boys."

"You may not read the boys' palms, or touch them in any manner. That is the condition of the Emperor," the old man corrected.

"Well, who would like to solve the problem then?" Krishna Deva Raya looked around at his courtiers. But they all sat with downcast eyes, not wanting to risk their reputation.

"What? Not one of my scholars has an answer for this puzzle?" Krishna Deva Raya thundered. "Will my friend's son return from my court unrecognised?"

"I don't think so," a voice spoke from the far corner of the court. Krishna Deva Raya looked up to see Tenali Rama standing with his hands folded. "I am confident I can recognise the royal heir. But meanwhile, should we not give these boys a royal welcome? After all, one of them is the Prince of Kalinga."

"By all means!" Krishna Deva Raya agreed wholeheartedly. "Get sweets and sherbets!" he ordered the servants.

When the boys were seated, Tenali Rama offered them sweets. One by one, each boy took a *laddu* from Tenali Rama. Then the court jester stepped back and turned to the minister from Kalinga.

"The second last boy is your Prince, O learned one."

Everyone was stunned. "How did you guess?" the old man asked curiously.

"I didn't guess. I found out."

"Well, how did you find out?" Krishna Deva Raya asked.

"When I gave the sweets to the boys, they all extended their hands to receive it, with their palms upturned. Except the boy here," Tenali patted the Prince's shoulder. "A prince does not know how to **take** things from anyone. His royal training forbids him from spreading his hands before anyone. He only knows how to **give** things to the needy. So he just stared."

The minister folded his hands. "I salute your genius, young man."

■ ■

Meeting God

Krishna Deva Raya was a deeply pious King. He began his mornings with an elaborate *pooja*, and encouraged religious discourses. He donated to religious charities, and built many beautiful temples in Vijayanagara, so that the other devotees too could worship the Lord.

One day, he decided to offer prayers at a temple along with his ministers. The temple was truly a work of art, and the statue of Lord Rama was so exquisite that the courtiers couldn't stop praising it. They all agreed that visiting the temple had been a divine experience.

"It was like meeting the Lord in person," said the Prime Minister.

Krishna Deva Raya was very pleased when he heard that. It was then that he noticed Tenali Rama standing aloof in a corner. He gazed at the statue of the Lord, and smiled mysteriously on hearing the Prime Minister's remarks.

"What is the matter, Tenali?" the King inquired. "Don't you agree with our Prime Minister?"

"I agree that it is truly a beautiful temple. But I don't think I can hope to meet God here."

The courtiers were aghast at Tenali's words. "Sacrilege!" they said. "If you cannot see the Lord in such pure surroundings, you can never hope to meet Him."

The King too was surprised by Tenali's answer. "Why do you say that Tenali?" he asked.

"Tonight, I will tell you, O King," Tenali answered mysteriously.

That night, on their usual visit to the city in disguise, Tenali Rama took the King to a shed outside the temple. It was dark except for a beam of light coming through an open window. "Look inside, My Lord," Tenali whispered.

When the King peeped inside, he saw the pious priest hurriedly completing his prayers. The King looked questioningly at Tenali, who explained, "The moment his prayers are over, he will drink liquor. This man collects money from devotees in the name of God, and then wastes it on liquor. If Lord Rama truly resided inside the temple, He would not allow such uncouth characters in His divine presence. The temple is very beautiful, no doubt, O King, but we can never hope to meet God by offering *dakshina* to a statue."

Krishna Deva Raya moved away from the window. "So is there no God?"

"We need to look elsewhere for God," Tenali led the King into an open field, where a farmer was returning from his fields after a hard day's work. "Look at this man who tills the land with his sweat. For him, work is worship. His land is his God."

The duo moved ahead, where a beautiful mansion was being built. Here, workers were breaking stones for the structure even as they dripped sweat. "Here too," Tenali said, "the workers are devoted to their work. For them, work is their God. That is why it is said that 'work is worship'."

The King was moved by Tenali's wisdom. "Yes Tenali! God is all-pervasive. He is not limited to temples and statues. Devotion to our work, and the people around us are the only way to meet Him."

■■

Time is Money

Late one afternoon, Krishna Deva Raya's soldiers dragged a simple-looking man into the court. The courtiers looked at his plain clothes and guilt-free face, and wondered why he was brought there. "Who is this man?" Krishna Deva Raya asked his soldiers.

"He is a criminal, My Lord," the soldiers responded.

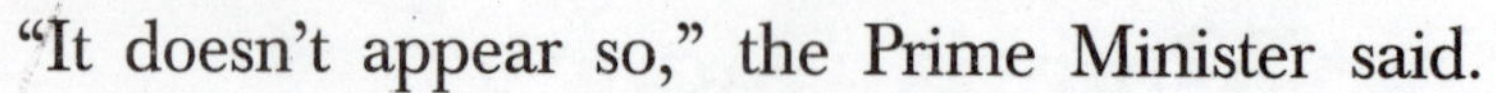

"It doesn't appear so," the Prime Minister said.

"Appearances can be deceptive, Sire. This shopkeeper was found cheating his customers this morning."

"I have done no such thing," the trader objected.

"How do you know he was cheating people?"

One of the soldiers stepped forward and folded his hands. "This morning, I had gone to the market on routine surveillance. On the way, I stopped near a shop. Inside, a customer and this shopkeeper were arguing loudly." The soldier paused for a moment. Then looking at the shopkeeper he continued. "I asked the customer what the matter was. He complained that this man was overcharging him."

"Well, where is the customer?" Krishna Deva Raya asked.

"Right here, O Lord." The soldiers pointed to another man who was accompanying them.

"Did this shopkeeper cheat you?"

"Yes Sire. This morning, I had gone to his shop to buy some rice," the man began. "He said that it would cost me 30 rupees for a kilogram. I checked the rice, and said that I was willing to give him 25 rupees. Hardly had I said that, when he immediately told me that I would now have to pay 35 rupees."

The King looked surprised. "Why is that?"

"That's what I asked him, Sire," the man said. "He replied that it would now cost me 40 rupees!"

"This is swindling!" the Prime Minister exclaimed.

"Yes! Yes!" the courtiers chorused. "He must be punished."

"We cannot allow such bad trading practices in the kingdom," the Prime Minister told Krishna Deva Raya. "Justice must be done."

"Justice must be done, O King," Tenali Rama spoke above the din in the court. "But with the trader."

The Prime Minister looked annoyed. "Do you not know the strict laws of Vijayanagara even after all these years, Tenali?" he asked. "Anyone found cheating must be punished."

Tenali looked at the King. "But I don't think this trader was cheating, O Lord."

"O yes? What was he doing then?"

"He was simply teaching his customers the value of time."

"Time? What has time got to do with rice?" the Prime Minister asked sarcastically.

"The shopkeeper told the customer how much a kilo of rice would cost. But the customer began haggling over the price, and wasted the trader's time."

"So?"

"So, My Lord," Tenali turned to face the King. "The merchant began adding the value of his time to the cost of the rice."

Krishna Deva Raya was intrigued. "Is that so?" he asked the trader.

"Yes, My Lord," the shopkeeper nodded. "Everyday, I have to deal with customers who try to bargain with me, despite the fact that I never overprice my goods. I end up wasting a lot of time with such customers. And time wasted is money lost. So now, I charge the customers for my time, if they haggle over the price."

Krishna Deva Raya laughed. "Set the man free!" he ordered his soldiers. Then he looked at the customer. "That's your lesson. Never waste time... Yours or anyone else's. It is the most valuable commodity in life. You can never get back the time you have lost."

The man lowered his head and paid the merchant 40 rupees for a kilo of rice and left the court quietly.

■ ■

The Greedy Thieves

Tenali Rama was an early sleeper. He usually had dinner at 8 o'clock, and soon afterwards went off to bed. His wife too put out all the lights early, and went to sleep. One such night, after 12 o'clock, Tenali woke up with a start. He thought he heard some noise. Sure enough, there were sounds coming from the courtyard behind the kitchen.

By now, his wife too was awake. "I think there are thieves in the house," she whispered.

"Don't worry dear, the thieves will never find anything in the house," Tenali Rama answered loudly in a confident voice.

His wife was surprised. "Why wouldn't they find anything? What about all the gold that the King keeps giving you as reward? And what about all your money? And my jewellery? And all the silver utensils?" she got somewhat hyper. "Do something. Call the neighbours... Light a lamp..."

Tenali turned over. "Relax my dear. I have safely stashed away all our gold and silver and money and your jewellery in the mango trees in the garden. No one knows about it. Don't worry. The thieves will not find anything in the house."

His wife thought for a moment, then asked in an even more worried tone. "But if you have hidden all our treasures in the mango trees, how can we give the contract for picking mangoes? What if the contractor finds everything and carries it off?"

"There is no way anyone can even spot the gold. I have hidden it so well. You should really stop worrying," so saying, Tenali changed sides and began snoring.

Now, the thieves had listened to the entire conversation. Upon learning that there was nothing to be stolen from the house, they quietly slipped out.

Early, the next day, four men came to Tenali's house. "Good morning, Sir. We are interested in the contract for mango picking in your garden," they said.

Tenali Rama realised they were the thieves who had broken into his house the night before. But he decided to play by their game. "Sure, why not!" he exclaimed. "But this year, keeping in mind the excellent yield of mangoes, I have decided that I will give the contract to whoever pays me five times the normal rate."

The thieves were taken aback. But they thought of the gold that Tenali had kept in the trees. So, they agreed.

For the next few days, they searched every mango tree in the garden. But the gold was nowhere to be found.

Disappointed, they realised that Tenali had probably never kept the gold in the trees at all. "Well, at least we can recover the extra money that we paid for the contract," said one of them.

So, they went to Krishna Deva Raya's court. "Justice, O King!" they knelt before the throne. "If courtiers like Tenali start looting people, where will poor men like us go?" they wailed.

"Tenali is looting people?" Krishna Deva Raya was surprised. "Tell me in detail."

So, the thieves revealed how Tenali had charged them **five** times the normal rate for picking mangoes in his grove. The King was angry. He summoned Tenali before him. "This is an unfair practice," he admonished the court jester.

Tenali listened to him, then he turned to the thieves. "If you were genuine contractors, you would have been able to value the mango yield correctly. And you would have never agreed to pay me five times more for the mango trees in my garden. It would not make any business sense to you." Then he turned to the King. "These men are thieves who broke into my house last week, and believing my claim that I had hidden my wealth in the mango trees, came disguised as contractors. To double check that my theory was right, I overcharged them."

On realising that their secret was out, the thieves begged for mercy. But, of course, the King sent them to prison. And praised his smart jester!

■ ■

Behind One's Back

One morning, just as Krishna Deva Raya entered the court, a messenger rushed in panting. "I have news for you, Sire," he exclaimed.

"Why don't you catch your breath while the King ascends the throne?" the Prime Minister interrupted him.

"It's a very disturbing piece of information, My Lord," the man protested.

"Let's hear it then," Krishna Deva Raya ordered.

"My Lord, last night, when I was returning home, it began raining suddenly. I was forced to take shelter near a washerman's house," the messenger lowered his eyes. "And I overheard him abusing Your Highness."

Krishna Deva Raya was livid with rage. "What?" he thundered. "Who is this man who dares insult the King? Soldiers! Arrest him now. And throw him in the darkest dungeon."

The soldiers were about to leave, when Tenali Rama spoke loudly. "Stop them, My Lord. The washerman is not to be blamed."

Krishna Deva Raya was furious. "Tenali! I will not tolerate just about any man maligning my good name."

Quietly, Tenali Rama looked up. "My Lord, do you think he is the only one?"

"You mean, you know others who insult their own King?"

"It's a human tendency to talk behind someone's back."

"I don't believe you."

"I will prove it to you, My Lord."

A few days later, Tenali Rama visited the King at night in disguise. "Come with me, Sire. We have a few places to visit."

The King knew that Tenali had planned something. So, without much ado, he set out with Tenali. Soon they reached the house of a high official from the government. "Sshhh!" Tenali signalled the King. In the silence of the night, the duo could hear voices from inside. The official was talking to his wife, and loudly criticising the King's actions.

"Come on!" Tenali whispered.

They moved on to a minister's residence. Like before, they stood quietly outside his window. Again, they heard vile remarks about the King. The story repeated itself every time they stopped outside a house and listened to the private conversations of residents.

Finally, they returned to the palace. "You heard yourself how people talk behind your back, My Lord," the jester said. "They are not to be blamed. It's human nature."

"But it's very upsetting, Tenali. Am I such a bad ruler?" Krishna Deva Raya said.

"The fault does not lie with you, O King," said the jester. "People will always gossip. What matters is that you don't let this tittle-tattle affect you and carry on with your good work."

"You are right," the King smiled at his dear friend.

■ ■

The Four Questions

The visitor stood in the middle of the court. "I have four questions, O King," his voice resonated throughout the hall. "I have travelled across eleven kingdoms. But I have not met **anyone** who can answer them in a logical sequence." He looked around the Vijayanagara court. "I hope I will not have to leave your court without my answers."

Krishna Deva Raya smiled confidently. "You will not be disappointed, learned one," he responded.

"Alright. My first question is, 'What will you do if, in a foreign city, you are faced with a hostile crowd that does not listen to anything that you say?' "

The courtiers thought for a while, then one of them said, "We will quietly leave the unfriendly place and return home."

The pundit smirked. "Unacceptable! That answer finishes the logical sequence of my questions."

The court fell silent on hearing this. What answer would give rise to the pundit's next question? No one could guess. Suddenly, Tenali Rama stood up. The pundit looked at him. "Yes?"

"So what if in a strange city the natives do not listen to me? At least they haven't abused me," Tenali answered the first question.

The pundit smiled. "What if they abuse you, insult you? What then?"

"I will be glad that they haven't hurt me physically."

"And if they start kicking and hitting you, then what would you do?"

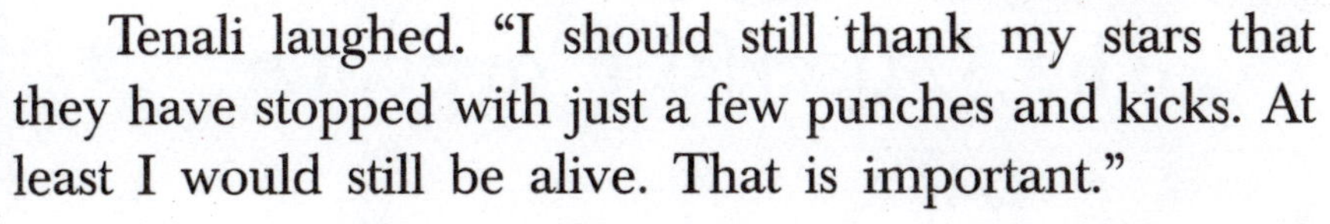

Tenali laughed. "I should still thank my stars that they have stopped with just a few punches and kicks. At least I would still be alive. That is important."

"You are doing well, jester. My fourth question is, what if these aggressive strangers take your life?"

Tenali bowed his head. "O learned one, I think I should be grateful to them for doing a deed of God. Thanks to them, my soul will be freed from its physical shackles, and can merge with the divine."

"Bravo!" the pundit exclaimed, even as the courtiers tried to make sense of the peculiar question-answer session. "Young man, your answers prove that apart from being extraordinarily intelligent, you also have the grit to survive in this world."

■ ■

The Miserly Carpenter

Every evening, Krishna Deva Raya visited the city to check whether his people were doing fine, and harboured no complaints. One such evening, he saw two small children sitting outside a house. They were so thin that their bones were visible. The King was appalled. He stopped the royal elephant, and sent Tenali Rama to ask who the children were, and whether they were orphans.

Soon Tenali returned with a man from one of the neighbouring houses. "Where are their parents?" the King asked.

"Their mother is ill," replied the man. "And their father has not returned from work."

"Their father must be a very poor man," the King observed. "Look at the children, they look so weak. Can he not afford to even feed them?"

"He is quite a well-to-do carpenter, My Lord," the neighbour said. "But he hates spending money. He never gives enough money to his wife to feed or clothe the children. He doesn't even buy her any medicines now that she is ill. He feels it's a waste."

Krishna Deva Raya couldn't believe that any man could be so mean to his own family. "We must punish this miser for his callous behaviour," he told Tenali Rama.

"Punishment may not be the cure for his attitude," said the jester. "But I know just how to change his mindset."

When they returned to the palace, Tenali ordered the soldiers to bring the children's father to him. Soon the man was brought before Tenali Rama. "Remove his clothes," Tenali instructed the soldiers.

"Hey! What are you doing?" the man protested. "Why are you removing my clothes? It is a cold night. I will freeze to death."

"Don't worry about the cold," Tenali told the miser. "My soldiers have lit a fire for you right there. That should keep you warm." He pointed to a small oil lamp in a corner.

The man looked at the flickering light. "Are you joking! That is no fire. It's not even enough to light up this room. Uh! Uhh!" His teeth were chattering by now.

Sternly, the court jester looked at the greedy man. "If your children can survive on a measly piece of bread that you give them once a day, and if your wife can recover from her illness without any medicines, why shouldn't the heat from this oil lamp keep you warm?"

The man gaped at Tenali Rama. He now understood why he was brought here! This was Tenali's way of ensuring the well-being of his family. "Have mercy on me, Sire," he fell on his knees. "I realise I have mistreated my own children. Forgive me!" He sobbed. "I will mend my ways and take good care of them."

Tenali Rama freed him and warned, "If I ever find that you are not providing for your children, there will be no mercy for you the next time."

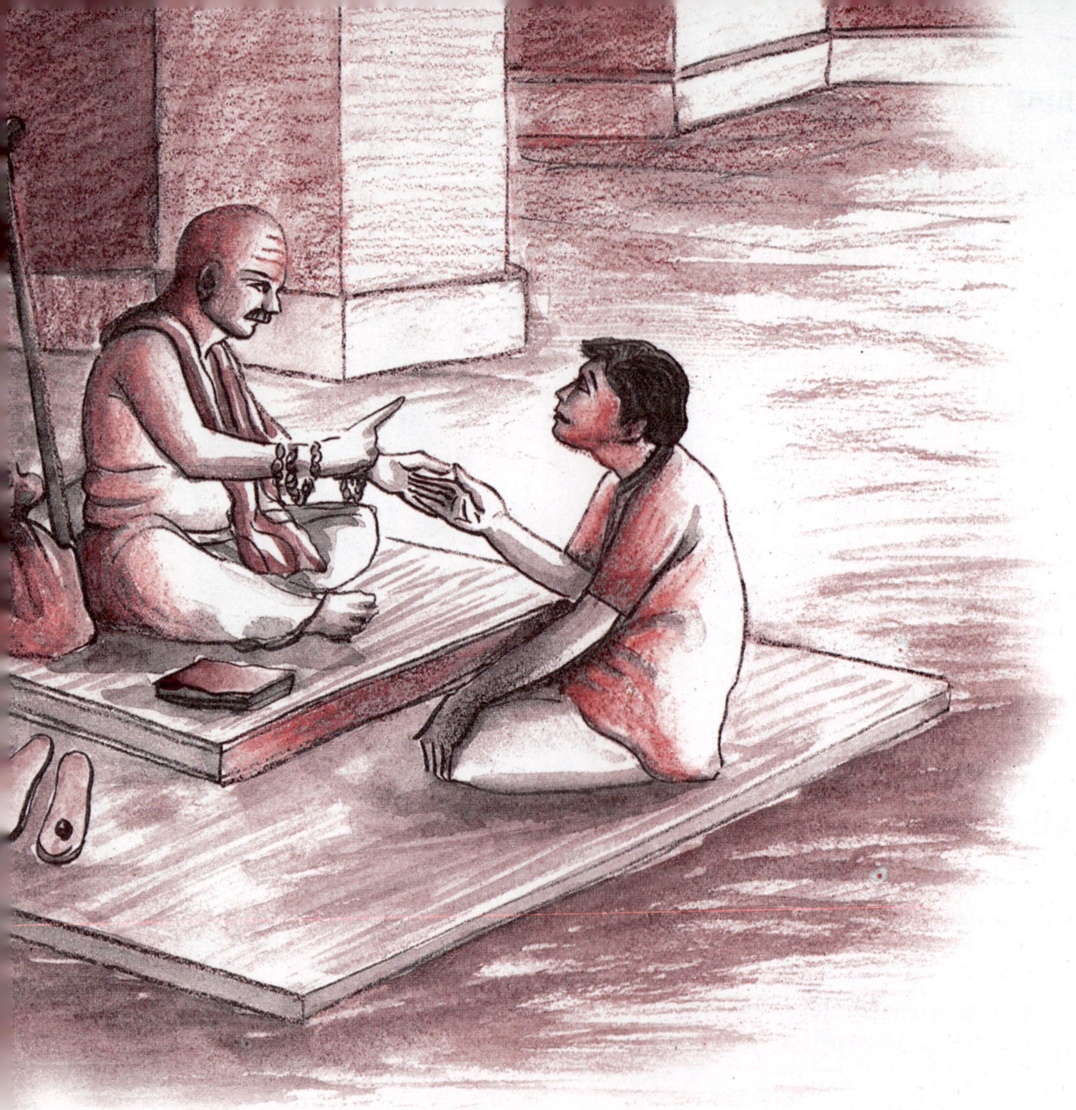

Destiny or *Karma*

One day, when Tenali Rama was walking home, he noticed a young man sitting before a roadside fortune-teller. Next to the fortune-teller was a small cage with a parrot. A few cards were spread on the pavement. The fortune-teller was reading a card that the parrot had picked up.

"Destiny has favoured you, son," he proclaimed. "Great opportunities await you. The King himself will honour you."

The young man perked up. Then he asked in a doubtful voice, "But how can I expect the King to honour me? I haven't done anything great. I am just a jobless person."

"Don't worry, son. Your planets will take care of this. It doesn't matter whether you work or not. Royal privileges are in store for you."

The young man was greatly pleased. He paid the fortune-teller handsomely, and went his way.

Now, Tenali Rama had listened to this conversation and decided to follow him. The young man entered a small house. From inside, Tenali could hear his old mother cough painfully. "Have you got my medicines, son?" she asked.

"I don't have any money," the man replied.

"Where will money come from if you don't work?"

"Don't be such a wet blanket, Amma," the young man replied insolently. "I am destined to receive royal honours. My planets say so. Soon, I will receive a lot of gold from the King, and then everything will be okay." So saying, he lay down on a cot and began daydreaming. His poor mother didn't know what to say.

Hearing this, Tenali Rama stopped a soldier passing by. "Arrest that man," he ordered. "And bring him to me tomorrow."

The next morning, the young man was duly presented before Tenali.

"Spare me, master," he begged. "I am just a poor man. What have I done that you should ask the soldiers to handcuff me and drag me to the court like this?"

Tenali ignored his pleas. "Three years in prison," he announced the sentence.

"Three years in prison?" the man howled. "I will die. At least tell me what I have done to deserve this!"

Tenali looked at him solemnly. "Well nothing. But your planetary position foretells that you should stay in the royal prison for the next three years."

"What?" the young man was shocked. "You are jailing me because of the planets? Is this a joke? Whoever heard of such foolishness?"

Tenali smirked. "Well… I don't see why not. After all, last night you refused to work because you expected fate to provide for you and your mother." He looked at the surprised man. "If planets can earn money for your mother's medicines, why can't those same planets put you in jail?"

The young man was dumbfounded. Tenali told him, "I will let you go this time. But remember that there is no alternative to hard work. Your destiny is never a substitute for *karma* – your deeds."

■■

Beggar's True Worth

One day, a beggar was found begging outside the King's palace. He was brought before the King. "Alms, O Merciful King!" He begged. Krishna Deva Raya took pity on the man and ordered his treasurer to give him 10 gold coins.

Tenali Rama had been observing the beggar carefully. On hearing the King's order, he interrupted, "My Lord, I too would like to give this beggar something."

The beggar couldn't believe his luck. "May you enjoy all the riches of life!" he blessed the jester.

"I will give him fifty gold coins," Tenali said and then paused. "But in return, he will have to give me something too."

"What can a beggar give you, Tenali?" Krishna Deva Raya was irritated.

Tenali turned to the beggar. "I will give you fifty gold coins, but you must let me cut off the little finger on your left hand."

The beggar was aghast. "No, no, master, I cannot allow that."

The King too was shocked. "Tenali, are you alright?"

Tenali ignored the King and tried to strike another bargain. "Alright, hundred gold coins, but I will cut off your left hand."

"Stop it Tenali!" the King snapped.

"Okay. How about two hundred gold coins for your right leg?"

The beggar was terribly frightened by now. "I cannot let you cut off my limbs, Sire."

"Oh, alright, then I have another deal. Five hundred gold coins for one eye."

The beggar began shivering. "I don't want your alms," he cried and tried to run away. But Tenali Rama held him back.

"You are getting greedy. I cannot give you more than a thousand gold coins, but I will take an eye, a ear and a limb. That's a deal."

The beggar didn't know how to escape this monster. "Save me, save me..." he begged the King.

"You fool... Don't you feel ashamed begging for money?" Tenali Rama looked at

the beggar in disgust. “God has blessed you with such a healthy body that you are not willing to give it up for even a thousand gold coins,” he reprimanded. “Have you understood your true worth now? Put these hands that you use only to beg to some fruitful work. And you will never have to fold them for alms again.”

The Real Culprit

"I am the culprit," one man said.

"No. I am the culprit," the other man protested. "You must hang me."

"He is lying!" the first man almost pushed the second fellow away. "I am the culprit. Hang me."

The Prime Minister sighed in frustration. "My Lord, what do we do? I have never seen anyone fight so much to go to the gallows."

"Call Tenali Rama," the King ordered.

When Tenali came, the entire episode was narrated to him.

"Even the Prime Minister has never seen such a strange case before," said a courtier.

"Hmmm... Let me see. These two brothers here claim that they are responsible for the killing of the thief."

"Yes, Sire," they both chorused.

"You say that the thief broke into your house after midnight, when you and your parents were fast asleep."

They nodded.

"And when your father woke up with the noise, the thief tried to strangle him."

They nodded again.

"That's when you awoke, and killed him to save your father."

"I killed him," said one.

"Don't listen to him. I killed him," the other replied. And they began arguing once again.

"Quite a complex case," Tenali observed. "Do you understand that the punishment for killing a man is death?"

They nodded solemnly.

"Alright. Take them away," Tenali ordered the soldiers. "We will know the real culprit tomorrow."

That night, the two brothers stayed awake arguing about who should take the blame for killing the thief. "You must not take the blame," said one. "I will not watch my younger brother die while I live on."

"You are the older son. If you die, whom will our father depend upon?"

"I killed the man. I am the culprit."

"I have always listened to you. Now it's your turn to do as I say. Let me go." They went on and on. Sometime in the night, another criminal was pushed into their cell. The two brothers kept their distance, whispering amongst themselves, and arguing. Long after everyone had fallen asleep, the sounds from their cell continued, as they still had not been able to decide who should take the blame.

The next morning, Tenali Rama came into the court. The brothers were brought before the King. "Yes, Tenali? Have you found the answer?"

"My Lord, the older brother has killed the thief," he stated confidently.

"And how can you be so sure?" the younger brother asked.

"Because I was the drunken criminal in your cell last night. I pretended to have passed out, but I was listening to all your arguments," Tenali smiled. "And I have never seen such love between two siblings. You are ready to die for your brother!"

Then he turned to the King. "My Lord, although we know that the older brother killed the thief, it was only to save their father." He looked at the brothers. "I recommend that he be set free."

The King agreed. And the brothers went home happily.

Artist's Impression

A celebrated artist was visiting the Vijayanagara court. Krishna Deva Raya had commissioned him to paint the Queen's portrait. After many weeks, the artist completed the life-like portrait. He brought it to the court for everyone to see. When he unveiled it, Krishna Deva Raya asked his courtiers, "How do you like it?"

"Hmmm… It's alright," the Prime Minister said. "But I think the artist has not been able to bring out the spark in the Queen's eyes."

"I think the bosom should have been wider," the *Rajguru* observed.

The hair, the lips, the colour of the dress... Everyone had something to say and an opinion to offer. The artist was very upset.

Now, Tenali Rama had been admiring the portrait for a while. He noticed how disappointed the artist looked. So, he turned to the King, and said, "I have a suggestion, My Lord."

"Yes?"

"Why don't we put the portrait in the city square? Thereby, even the citizens can suggest changes. Then the artist can redraw a better portrait."

"That's a very good idea," said Krishna Deva Raya, and the portrait found itself in the city square. Now even passers-by could pick up a brush and point out a mistake. Soon the whole painting was

disfigured. Nothing remained of the likeness that the artist had portrayed. When the canvas was brought to the court after a week, the artist was heartbroken to see his piece of art ruined.

Nonetheless, he made another portrait of the Queen. This time it was even better than the last one. After a few weeks, when he presented it to the court, Tenali Rama said, "Last time, we allowed everyone to point out the mistakes, My Lord. Now why don't we let them appreciate the good features of this portrait?"

So once again, the portrait found itself in the city square. 'Please highlight the feature that you think is the bes', a board next to it read.

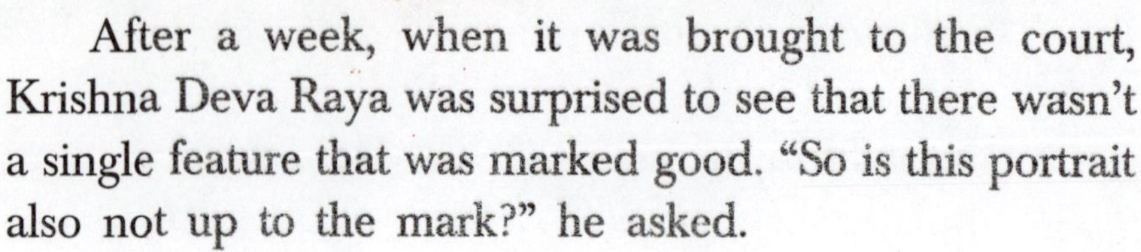

After a week, when it was brought to the court, Krishna Deva Raya was surprised to see that there wasn't a single feature that was marked good. "So is this portrait also not up to the mark?" he asked.

"There is nothing wrong with the portrait, My Lord," Tenali said. "What's wrong is people's attitude. Ask them to find faults, and they will readily point out a mistake where there is none. But ask them to cite a good point, and they will never be able to find one."

The King realised that he had wronged the artist by letting everyone criticise his work.

■ ■

Who's Worthy of These Flowers?

It was the beginning of spring. Krishna Deva Raya and his courtiers were strolling through the royal garden. The exquisite blooms with their intoxicating fragrance had everyone mesmerised. "These divine creations truly belong in a temple," the Prime Minister observed.

"For us, the King is God. These flowers would look better on the royal crown," another courtier added.

"I think they would look better as garlands adorning the delicate wrists of a beautiful maiden," Krishna Deva Raya smiled and said.

"Hear! Hear!" the courtiers chorused in unison. "Our King really has an eye for beauty. Trust him to think of such an appropriate place for these lovely flowers."

Tenali Rama heard all this talk. But he just smelt the flowers and walked on quietly.

"Looks like Tenali has other thoughts. As usual," the courtiers sniggered.

Tenali stopped in his tracks. "If I had my way, I would strew these flowers on the road where the brave warriors of our kingdom walk."

"What an idea!" everyone laughed. "So you want these blooms to be crushed under the rough feet of soldiers."

Tenali was unperturbed. "My Lord, our ancestors believed that the motherland occupies a status higher than even the heavens. That means the soldier who protects my motherland is just as sacred to me. And what better place for these pretty blossoms than his feet?"

Krishna Deva Raya couldn't help appreciating Tenali's patriotism.

■ ■

Mum's the Word

Tenali Rama's neighbour was a very quarrelsome man. He always quarrelled with his wife, fought with colleagues at work, argued with friends, ticked off the children... It had got so bad that everyone began to avoid him. He had made his own life miserable.

One day, walking past Tenali Rama's house, he bumped into the witty jester. Tenali smiled at him. "Hello, how are you?" he asked.

"I am in a terrible situation," the neighbour confessed.

"What's the matter?"

The man told Tenali the whole story. "So you see, I just don't seem to be able to have a normal conversation with anyone any longer. I am always shouting at people, fighting with them, abusing them... I try very hard to control my temper, but it seems to have got the better of me. Every time I open my mouth, angry words tumble out."

Tenali looked at him thoughtfully. “That is a very serious problem. But don’t worry. I have a remedy for that!” So saying, he went inside the house, and brought a quaint bottle. “This is a rare medicine that my Guru once gave me. It has a calming effect on the mind.”

Tenali gave his neighbour the bottle. “Whenever you get into an argument, just take a sip from this bottle, but mind you, don’t swallow it. Keep it in your mouth till the other person has finished talking. After five minutes, you can spit out the medicine. Do this for six months. And things will change.”

The neighbour thanked Tenali and went off. Six months later, he called on Tenali Rama again. “Your medicine has worked wonders. I haven't fought with my wife since the day you prescribed the medicine. I haven't scolded my children, and I no longer get into arguments with my friends. It's an amazing medicine!" he gushed. "But I have finished it all now, and I fear that my temper will return. Can you give me some more of it?"

Tenali began laughing. "Dear friend that was just plain water."

"Plain water?"

"Yes, your problem was that you couldn't control the urge to argue, and then you lost your temper. But for the past six months, whenever there was a row, you sipped the water and obviously couldn't talk even if someone was squabbling with you," he guffawed. "Since you didn't speak, you didn't lose your temper. And a one-sided argument cannot go on and on. So, soon there were no fights at all."

The neighbour simply gaped at Tenali Rama. "Was it that simple?"

"Yes, my friend. If you want to avoid arguments, just keep mum. Life will be very peaceful."

■ ■

The Magic Key Ring

The magician was exceptionally gifted. He entertained Krishna Deva Raya and his ministers with extraordinary tricks. When his act was over, the court broke into loud applause. "Ask what you want," Krishna Deva Raya said. "And you will not be refused."

The magician bowed before the King. "I don't want riches, O King. I just seek the answer to a trick that a child once conjured up for me, and which I could never solve."

The courtiers were surprised. "What? A gifted magician like you couldn't do a simple trick that a child devised?"

The magician shook his head. "No, Sire. I have been to many kingdoms and asked many scholars, but no one has been able to help me. I came to Vijayanagara hoping that someone from your court would be able to solve the problem for me."

"What is it?" Krishna Deva Raya asked.

The magician produced a small key ring. "Who can slip through this ring?"

"How can a grown man slip through a key ring?" the courtiers protested. "Besides, we are not magicians. We don't know how to do magic."

"Well... someone will have to think of an answer," said Krishna Deva Raya. "That's his reward."

When no one responded for a long while, Tenali Rama stood up. "Permit me to try, My Lord," he told the King.

Then he walked up to the magician. "Can I have a look at the key ring?"

"Sure!" the magician looked pleased. He had heard of Tenali Rama and his quick wit.

Tenali took the key ring in his hand and turned it around, once... twice... thrice. Then he produced a piece of paper and wrote his name on it. He showed it to the magician. "Can you read it?"

The magician read: "TENALI RAMA".

"Right!" said Tenali, and rolled up the piece of paper. Then he held it up for all to see. "I hope you all heard it... That was TENALI RAMA."

And then, he passed the roll of paper through the key ring. "There! Tenali Rama has slipped through the ring!"

The applause this time was even louder than before. The magician had received his answer.

■ ■

Heaven and Hell

One day, all the ministers were chatting amongst themselves. The topic veered towards heaven. "Only if you are pious and donate generously to temple charities can you ever hope to go to heaven," they all felt.

"I don't agree with you," Tenali Rama broke in.

"When do you agree with anyone?" jeered Swami, a particularly jealous courtier.

Tenali ignored him, and continued. "I believe that heaven and hell both exist right here on earth." Everyone laughed. Whoever had heard of heaven on earth? Or hell either?

But Krishna Deva Raya, who was listening to the conversation, said, "Tenali, that is an arguable statement to make. Can you show us heaven or hell on earth?"

"Sure, My Lord," Tenali agreed. "I can tell you how to look for it. But everyone has to find it for himself."

"Well, who will go first?"

Upon hearing the King's words, everyone moved backwards. So, Tenali spoke up. "Why don't we send Swami?"

Swami was irritated, but couldn't say no. "So how do I go about it?" he asked reluctantly.

“You need to go through the city, disguised of course,” Tenali said.

“Disguised as what?”

“Oh, anything. A beggar maybe!” The courtiers laughed.

Swami was really annoyed now. But he had no choice. So, he dressed in some rags, and with a stone bowl in hand, set out across the city. For an entire day, he roamed on the streets. In the evening when he returned, he was tired and hungry.

“Well, did you find either heaven or hell?” the King asked.

“What heaven? What hell? I didn’t see any such thing. Tenali has been lying through his teeth. He did this because he doesn’t like me. I roamed the whole day, and all I have to show is some stale bread and some copper coins,” he replied angrily.

"Cool down brother," Tenali tried to calm him. "You say you didn't see heaven nor hell. But you must have seen other things during the day."

"Of course!" Swami snapped. "I saw a husband beating his wife, I saw their children crying... Oh, my head still hurts from all that racket!"

"What else did you see?"

"I saw another couple with their old parents. They were kind enough to share their lunch with me."

"So you did see heaven and hell," Tenali proclaimed. "Families where you saw love and kindness, that was heaven. But places where there was nothing except anger, resentment, violence and grief, those families had created their own hell."

The courtiers couldn't but agree!

■■

Truth as You See It

One day, Tenali Rama came home to find his neighbour's sons fighting heatedly outside the house. They were arguing so loudly that you could hear their voices right up to the last house in the street. Now, Tenali Rama was very fond of these boys, who were twins. So, he went up to them and asked, "Hey! What's the matter?"

The twins turned to their neighbour. "Who is older between the two of us?" asked Mani.

"I told him I am the older one," said Chintamani. "But he just doesn't want to listen."

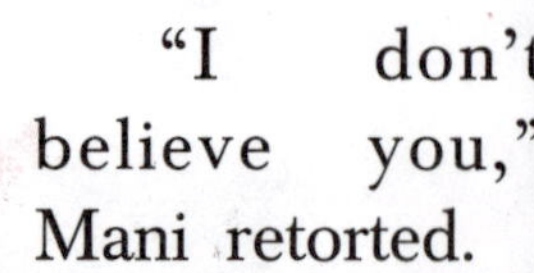

"I don't believe you," Mani retorted.

"Why won't you? If mother told you that I am the older one, and if father also told you the same thing, why won't you believe it?" The twins began fighting again.

"Stop! Stop!" Tenali separated them. "I have an idea. Let's see who is older between the two of you. Get me a bottle and two marbles."

Mani ran to fetch the marbles and Chintamani brought a bottle. "Great! Now each of you take a marble. Chintamani says he is older because he was the first to be born. Right?"

"Right!" said Chintamani.

"Okay, so we will give him the benefit of doubt and allow him to put his marble in the bottle first," so saying, Tenali put Chintamani's marble inside the bottle. "Now Mani, where is your marble?" This marble also went inside the bottle.

"Alright! Now we will turn the bottle over, and see who comes out first!"

However, the bottle had a narrow mouth and only one marble could come out first. Since Mani's marble was on top, it was the first to emerge.

"Looks like we have a problem here!" said Tenali. "Chintamani was the first to go in, because he is the older twin. But he cannot come out first, because of Mani. Do you understand?" The twins looked confused.

So Tenali explained. "Although Chintamani was the first twin to emerge from your mother's womb, he didn't go in first. Mani was inside first. But he could come out only after Chintamani, who came in later."

Mani laughed. "So if I say I am the older one because I went in first, then I am right."

Chintamani laughed too. "And if I say I am the older one because I came out first, then I am right too."

"Exactly!" Tenali Rama had solved the problem. The twins never fought again.

■■

Tales of **Gopal** the jester

Full of Wit, Wisdom & Humour

In ancient times, the jester was a very important person because he could always make people laugh and be happy. Many humorous tales are attributed to these jesters. There are stories of Birbal, patronised by Emperor Akbar, of Tenali Ramakrishna, from the court of Krishna Deva Raya of south India, and of Gopal, the chief jester in the court of Maharaja Krishna Chandra of Bengal.

Maharaja Krishna Chandra ruled during the Islamic period in medieval India. His biggest rival was the governor of Murshidabad, referred to as 'the Nawab' in all the stories. One is not sure about who the Nawab actually was. He could very well have been a fictitious character created to make the stories interesting. Indeed, neither the Maharaja nor the Nawab is depicted as really intelligent. Many stories are told of how the Maharaja tries to outwit the Nawab and how Gopal assists in these endeavours. In every story, it is Gopal who emerges the hero.

Animals and birds enliven our world. Since all creatures have their own unique appearance, man has wondered how many of these came to be. The imaginative stories he wove to explain these passed into folklore throughout the world. How the tiger acquired stripes, how the crocodile got its rough, scaly back, why the dog barks at and chases everyone it sees... and other interesting animal stories.

The tales in this book come from all corners of the globe – North America, Africa, Europe, Australia, South-east Asia and our own beautiful land India – and bring us glimpses of faraway lands.